RIVER LIFE

*Using a net, a man tests his luck
in the rich waters of the Amazon.*

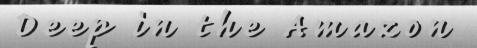

RIVER LIFE

by James L. Castner

BENCHMARK BOOKS

MARSHALL CAVENDISH
NEW YORK

With thanks to Dr. Gary Hartshorn, Organization for Tropical Studies, Duke University, for his careful review of the manuscript.

Benchmark Books
Marshall Cavendish Corporation
99 White Plains Road
Tarrytown, New York 10591-9001
www.marshallcavendish.com

• • •

Library of Congress Cataloging-in-Publication Data
Castner, James L.
River Life / James L. Castner
p. cm—(Deep in the Amazon)
Includes bibliographical references (p.).
Summary: Describes the geology, topography, and fishes of the Amazon River Region.
ISBN 0-7614-1127-5
1. Natural history—Amazon River Watershed—Juvenile literature.
[1. Natural history—Amazon River Region.   2. Amazon River.]   I. Title.
QH112 .C37 2002   577.6′4′09811—dc21   99-057015

• • •

Printed in Hong Kong
1 3 5 7 8 6 4 2

• • •

Book Designer: Judith Turziano
Photo Research: Candlepants Incorporated

• • •

CREDITS
Cover photo: *Photo Researchers Inc.* / Francois Gohier
The photographs in this book are used by permission and through the courtesy of;
Corbis: Buddy Mays, 2–3; Layne Kennedy, 8; Wolfgang Kaehler, 10; Yann Arthus-Bertrand, 20; Jay Dickman, 24;
Kevin Schafer, 29; Richard List, 52; Charles & Josette Lenares, 54; *Photo Researchers Inc.*: Francois Gohier,12;
David S. Frazier Photo Library, 14; David Schleser, 16; Will and Deni McIntyre, 18, 22; Steinhart Aquariums, 32, 40;
Mark Smith, 36 (lower); Jim Zipp, 38; M. Wendler Lokapia, 41; Art Wolfe, 42; Jacques Jangoux, 44.
Michael Goulding: 27 (top and bottom); *Animals Animals/Earth Scenes*: Gouldng-Partri OSF, 30;
Nigel J.H. Smith, 36 (top), 56; N. Gordon Surv–OSF, 50. Dr. James L. Castner, 34, 46, 48.

CONTENTS

AUTHOR'S NOTE

On several occasions I have flown over the Amazon rain forest in a single engine float plane with the door removed to get a better view. From high above, one part of this endless expanse of green did not appear to differ much from another. It was obvious that I was looking at many different kinds of trees, yet the forest as a whole seemed to be one continuous mass. It was divided only by brown, curving rivers that sometimes looked silver with the light reflected from the sun.

But the impression that all of the Amazon forest is the same—or that even the rivers of the basin are similar— could not be more wrong. This is a region full of variety and change. The rivers are the lifelines of the basin, sustaining and shaping the land around it. They rise, overflowing their banks and spreading onto the floodplain. They help support the great biodiversity found here.

The rivers of the basin can be divided in three main types, each with its own rhythms and distinct life-forms. To explore them, we will not need a plane, though. Let's take a boat ride instead through these fascinating underwater worlds.

BEAN SEA

ATLANTIC OCEAN

VENEZUELA

GUYANA

SURINAME

FRENCH GUIANA

Bogotá

LOMBIA

Japurá River

Negro River

Equator

tumayo River

o River

Upper Amazon

Middle Amazon

Lower Amazon

Manaus

Marajó

quitos

Leticia

Tefé

Santarém

Tocantins R.

Tapajós River

Xingu River

Madeira River

Ucayali River

allpa

PERU

BOLIVIA

BRAZIL

Amazon River Basin

0   400 miles

0   600 kilometers

AN

The Amazon is the longest and largest river on Earth. Here a canoeist appears to be plying the waters of an ocean or a giant lake, not a river.

Chapter One

FLOWING THROUGH TIME

T he pulsing heart of the Amazon rain forest is the rambling Amazon River, the longest and the largest in the world. Originating high in the Andes Mountains of Peru, the 4,000-mile-long (6,437-km) Amazon River flows almost due east until it empties into the Atlantic Ocean on the northeastern coast of Brazil. At its mouth, the Amazon becomes so wide that its waters completely surround Marajó, an island about the size of Switzerland. Nearly one-fifth of all the Earth's freshwater flows through the rivers and streams of the Amazon Basin. If all of its navigable waterways were measured, they would add up to more than 50,000 miles (80,467 km).

Today, the river lies at the center of a vast region. The basin is flanked by the Andes Mountains, whose sharp peaks line the western coast of South America. Forming the basin's northern and southern rim are the ancient rock formations the Guiana Shield and the Brazilian Shield. Thus only in the east where its path is clear can the Amazon flow to the sea.

The Age of Glaciers

But this has not always been the case. If we could travel back in time more than 15 million years to the geological period called the Miocene, this part of South America would look like an entirely different place. The Andes Mountains have not yet formed, and the land is flat all the way to the western shore. A much smaller Amazon River flows west, not east,

*The mighty Amazon begins as tiny trickles on the damp,
forested slopes of the Andes Mountains. Rock and soil particles
from these mountains are carried by the current and add to the
fertility of flooded lands thousands of miles downstream.*

into the Pacific Ocean somewhere along the coast of Ecuador or Peru. The great Brazilian and Guiana Shields form a blockade, a wall of rock to the north, south, and east, joining near the present-day city of Santarém, Brazil. The vast low-lying plain contained within these mountainous shields is dotted with countless lakes.

The Miocene epoch saw great changes in the South American landscape. Geologic pressures within the earth led to movements in its crust. Rocks were lifted and folded in the process, giving rise to the Andes mountain range. The creation of this great mountainous wall blocked the course of the Amazon and other rivers that flowed west. Now completely enclosed, these rivers had nowhere to flow and thus pooled, forming an immense lake that filled the entire basin. The lake did not remain however. During the Pleistocene Era, which began 2 million years ago and lasted to about 11,000 B.C, a break in the eastern portion of the shield allowed this massive reserve of water to flow to the Atlantic.

But the transformation of the continent was not complete. Throughout its long history, the Earth has experienced a series of ice ages, during which colder weather has caused huge sheets of ice to form over much of the land. The advance and retreat of these enormous glaciers have resulted in a constant shift in the level of the oceans. When the ice sheets last melted, about 13,000 years ago, the oceans rose, and the Amazon plain was once again flooded. These floodwaters carried soil particles and sediments that eventually settled and were deposited along the plain. It is these sediments that make up the soil of the Amazon Basin.

The Amazon is more than just a single channel of water. During the flood season, the border between land and water becomes blurred. Millions of gallons spill over the banks and spread into the surrounding forest. The river comes to the land, creating a soggy world for the plants and animals that live along the floodplain. They have learned to adapt to these conditions in which water can cover much of the plain for months. The cycle of flooding is an ancient pattern that nourishes the rain forest and challenges its residents to this day.

In a vast and densely forested region where there are no highways, travel by boat is often a necessity. With thousands of intersecting waterways, rivers are the roads of the Amazon Basin.

Chapter Two

DIVIDING THE RIVERS

*L*et's hire a boat and trace the course of this mighty waterway and the three types of rivers we will find threading the basin— black, white, and clear. We'll start at the headwaters, or the place where a river begins. For the Amazon they are located high in the Andes Mountains of Peru. Water from precipitation and melting snow comes together pouring down the mountainside to form streams of ever-increasing size. These streams join and in many cases become powerful rivers in their own right. The two rivers debated by geographers to be the source of the Amazon are the Marañón and the Ucayali. They come together near the city of Iquitos, Peru. Their confluence, or the place where they join, marks the official point at which the name *Amazon* is used. The Amazon River is so deep and wide at the city of Iquitos that large oceangoing cargo ships can reach this river port even though it is more than 2,000 miles (3,219 km) inland.

As the Amazon continues its eastward flow, it passes through an area called *tres fronteras*, which in Spanish means "three borders." This is where the countries of Peru, Colombia, and Brazil share a border. From this point on, the Amazon River is contained entirely within Brazil. During the first half of its Brazilian course—from the Peruvian border to the jungle metropolis of Manaus—the river is often referred to by its Portuguese name, the Solimões. From Manaus east to the river's mouth, it is called by its more familiar name, the Amazon.

The Amazon River is often divided into upper, middle, and lower regions. The Upper Amazon is that section of the river and basin to the west (or upriver) of the Brazilian town of Tefé. This city is approximately midway between the Peruvian border and Manaus in north-central Brazil. Thus a large portion of western Brazil and almost all of the Amazon Basin found in Bolivia, Peru, Ecuador, Colombia, and Venezuela are considered the Upper Amazon. The Middle Amazon is almost completely Brazilian, contained between Tefé and the city of Santarém. The Lower Amazon stretches east (or downstream) of Santarém to the river's mouth at the coast.

Beyond the divisions of the great river itself, the Amazon is fed by a network of tributaries, large rivers and tiny streams that flow from the north and south. These waterways can be divided into three general categories based on the color and clarity of the water. We can thus refer to whitewater, blackwater, and clearwater rivers. Whitewater is the category to which the Amazon itself belongs. It is a word that means different things to different people. Have you ever gone rafting or canoeing on a swiftly flowing river? The water surges and crashes, sometimes flinging the boat as if it were a toy. Although the Amazon has its share of rapids, that is not the reason it is considered a whitewater river. Instead, it is its relatively clear waters that give the river this distinction.

When compared to a blackwater river, there is a noticeable difference in the color of a whitewater river. Nowhere is this more evident than where the Amazon and the Negro meet at Manaus. Their waters flow side by side for a great distance, and when viewed from the air it is easier to understand why the light brown waters of the Amazon could be considered "white" next to the dark, opaque waters of the Negro.

Other major whitewater rivers are the Napo and Putumayo in Peru and the Madeira in Brazil. The whitewater rivers have their headwaters in the Andes. The nutrient-rich sediments and dissolved minerals they pick up from the mountains produce their muddy, creamy colors. These sedi-

Near the city of Manaus in Brazil, the dark water of the blackwater river the Negro mingle with the muddy brown water of the Amazon. Although the sediments in the Amazon give it a light brown appearance, it is classified as a whitewater river due to its somewhat lighter color.

ments, which are suspended in the river water, are of crucial importance to the rivers' animal life. They also help to keep the floodplain fertile year after year. The rich soil that is annually deposited on the floodplain allows the inhabitants to grow their crops.

Blackwater rivers have been more accurately named, given their dark, tea-colored appearance. The headwaters of these rivers are found in the

Blackwater rivers, such as the Curaray in Peru, have a dark or tea-colored appearance. The river is tinted by the tannins and organic chemicals that leach into the water.

sandy, heavily weathered Guiana and Brazilian Shields. Thus they are acidic and nutrient poor, carrying very little sediment in their waters. Nearly all the nutrients were leached out of the shields long ago, so the soils that come from them are practically sterile. Tannins and organic chemicals do not bind to these sandy soils. Instead they dilute in the water and give the rivers their dark color. Blackwater rivers are found in the central and western regions of Amazonia. In addition to the Negro, they include the Jaú, Preto, Zamula, and Cuiuni.

Clearwater is the third type of river. These rivers also originate in the Brazilian and Guiana Highlands. They are slightly acidic and like the blackwater rivers, they are very low in nutrients. But for reasons not fully understood they do not pick up the organic chemicals that darken the water. This is why their waters tend to have, as their name suggests, a clearer appearance. Because clearwater rivers are low in nutrients, aquatic plants tend not to thrive in them. They do draw diverse animal life, though, from the flooded forests beyond the banks. The largest clearwater rivers include the Tapajós, the Xingu, and the Tocantins and are found in the southern region of the Lower Amazon.

The seasonal change in the level of the basin's rivers can be drastic. Only weeks earlier the bases of these trees were underwater. The dark stains on the trunks show how high the water reached.

Chapter Three

FLOODING THE BANKS

espite their different colors and origins, all of the rivers of the Amazon Basin share one extremely important trait—their seasonal change in water level. For thousands of years the rivers have flooded for several months of the year. The water level in larger Amazonian rivers typically rises as much as 20 to 40 feet (6.1–12.2 m) in a season. These changes are the result of rainfall and snowmelt—the combined precipitation of a drainage area the size of the United States.

Rainfall in the Amazon Basin varies from place to place, but the annual average is from 60 to 120 inches (1.5–3 m). Flooding does not occur at the same time throughout the basin because the seasons of heaviest rainfall vary throughout the region. The Amazon Basin covers an enormous area spanning almost 25 degrees of latitude, or more than 772,000 square miles (2,000,000 sq km). The equator runs through the region, but divides it unevenly with more of the basin lying south of the dividing line. Thus the periods of maximum rainfall tend to be months apart. Northern rivers such as the Negro reach maximum water levels around June. Southern rivers such as the Xingu and the Madeira tend to peak around March. Because the northern and southern rivers do not flood at the same time, the nearby forests can be saturated for long periods of time. Certain low-lying areas of forest may be covered in water for as long as eight to ten months of the year.

Underwater Forests

Although many types of forests thrive in the basin, it is the floodplain habitats that are most affected by the seasonal floods. Flooded forests grow on the floodplains of Amazonian rivers and are often called flood-

*Forests are flooded during certain periods of the year
when the Amazon and other rivers overflow their banks.
Armed with a variety of adaptations, these trees are able
to survive the soggy conditions of their world.*

plain forests, seasonally flooded forests, or seasonally inundated forests. When water is at its highest level, most of the floodplain is submerged beneath 5 to 25 feet (1.5–7.6 m) of water. Flooded forests make up only about 2 to 3 percent of the total forest in the Amazon Basin. This is still a huge area, equal to about twice that of England.

In the Amazon Basin there are two types of flooded forests: *várzea* and *igapó*. *Várzea* forests are found on the floodplains of whitewater rivers such as the Amazon, Napo, and Madeira. A wealth of fish and other aquatic life can be found among the huge trees. *Igapó* forests grow near blackwater and clearwater rivers. Since their waters carry few nutrients, the aquatic life they harbor is less extensive, although the number of terrestrial species rivals those found in *várzea* forests.

It is easy to think of the rivers, lakes, and forests of the Amazonian lowlands as distinct and separate, yet this is not so. Actually a river along with its floodplain forests and lakes forms a single, unified system that undergoes seasonal changes. For as the rivers flood their banks, the water joins the forest, creating a new world that is both aquatic and terrestrial. Lakes may become completely inundated, only to reappear when the waters recede. Leaf litter that once made up the forest floor becomes a vast lakebed instead. Fish and dolphins swim around exposed roots and the bases of trees that were previously the home of terrestrial species.

For people, floods are often disastrous. But the plants and animals of the Amazon Basin are well adapted to these seasonal changes. For many organisms, especially fish, it is a time of plenty. They are granted access to new habitats. The flooded forest greatly expands the area in which they can forage for a bounty of new seeds, fruits, insects, and detritus. Food during this season is so plentiful that some fish build up enough fat to last them through the low-water season when they remain in the river channels. As for the nonaquatic organisms, many already live in the trees or easily adjust to an arboreal way of life. Often, they simply move higher up, farther from the forest floor. In the case of strictly terrestrial animals,

As waters rise and spread into the surrounding forest,
fish and other aquatic animals gain access to vast new habitats
in which they can hunt or forage. For these organisms,
high-water season is a time of plenty.

they seek higher ground and migrate to the terra firma forests, which are not affected by the floods.

It is the plants and trees of the floodplain that are most impacted by the sudden rush of water. They cannot pick up and move like the animals do. Instead they become partially covered and in many cases completely submerged for months at a time. Yet they too have adapted to these apparently extreme conditions. Some species have what are called respiratory

roots, which grow above the water level. These allow the tree to receive the oxygen it needs. Other trees in the flooded forest have developed buttress roots. These are huge, wall-like structures that sometimes stick out from the base of a tree like the fins on a rocket. They may extend 25 to 30 feet (8–9 m) from the trunk, bulging out in a snakelike fashion until they reach the ground.

One such tree showing this unusual adaptation is the giant ceiba or kapok tree. A mature ceiba tree may tower 100 to 125 feet (30–40 m) above the ground. They are easy to identify because of their huge trunks and massive horizontal branches that cluster at the top to form the crown. In order to support such heights, the trees need sturdy bases, especially when the soil is saturated or soggy. Unfortunately, these towering ceibas are prized by logging companies, and few of these buttressed giants exist today.

The majority of trees in seasonally flooded forests grow fairly quickly. Essentially, they make the most of the time they have for growing. Some trees are granted only two or three months of the year when their bases are not submerged. This adds another degree of difficulty to the trees' need to adapt. The plants of the floodplain must be able to tolerate both wet and dry conditions. The trees of the terra firma forest are free of these pressures. They are too far from the floodplain for the waters to reach them. If the floods ever did, few would survive.

Riding in an open boat provides a great opportunity to see some of the of creatures that live in and around the river. The Amazon provides the ideal conditions for a bounty of fish to thrive in its waters.

Chapter Four

TWO SCHOOLS

T here are more species of freshwater fish found in the rivers and lakes of the Amazon Basin than anywhere else in the world. More than 1,700 species have been recorded, but that is probably barely half of the actual number living here. Scientists estimate that as many as 3,000 species ply the basin's waterways. In comparison, the Zaire River (the second largest in the world) has fewer than 600 species, while the Mississippi River has only about 250, or one-tenth of those found in Amazonian waters. So, what has led to this astounding assortment of fish?

As we have seen, all water is not the same. In addition to the three main types of rivers, the basin is also home to countless other bodies of water. Ponds, lakes, streams, swamps, and estuaries are just a few. This great variety of aquatic habitats has led to an extremely diverse number of organisms. Each habitat provides different conditions in which a great number of species can thrive. In addition, the seasonal floods make this watery territory even larger.

The vast majority of fish in the New World fall into two main groups: the catfish and the characins. These two groups represent more than 80 percent of all species found in the Amazon Basin and a majority of the food fish consumed by its residents. More than one thousand species of catfish are found in the rivers and lakes of South America. They range in size from tiny, blood-sucking parasites no more than 1 inch (2.5 cm) long to riverine giants such as the piraíba longer than a full-grown person and weighing more than 200 pounds (110 kg). Catfish are smooth and scaleless and have narrow, dangling, whiskerlike structures (for which they are named) around the mouth called barbels. Many catfish have a flat underside, although this does not necessarily mean that they are bottom dwellers. Some larger Amazonian catfish are heavily pigmented with striped patterns and have barbels that extend half the length of their body. The barbels are sense organs that have evolved as an adaptation to an environment where visibility is poor. Along with providing the catfish's sense of touch, the barbels are covered with taste buds as well.

Two of the largest Amazonian catfish are the dourada (dew-RAH-duh) and the piramutaba (PEER-uh-moo-TAH-buh). They belong to a large family of catfish called the pimelodids, which have evolved a variety of interesting feeding behaviors. They capture prey by opening their mouths and quickly sucking in huge gulps of water. The smaller prey fish, along with any other nearby material, is drawn in and swallowed whole. It is a successful strategy. Both these species are migratory, and along with other predatory members of this family are abundant in the basin's rivers. Of all the fish found in the basin, they are the leading predators.

The dourada is a sleek, silver-headed catfish with a golden tint to its body and a sharklike appearance. As an adult, it may weigh from 50 to 60 pounds (22.7–27.2 kg) and grow up to 6 feet (1.8 m) in length. Its success as a species throughout the Amazon Basin is linked to its ability to flourish in all three river types.

Its migration cycle, which spans the full length of the Amazon, can take several years to complete. Young dourada leave the estuaries of the Lower Amazon and swim upstream to the Middle Amazon. Here they disperse into the various rivers where they spend from one to two years feeding and growing. When they have matured, they migrate upstream once again to the whitewater rivers of the Upper Amazon, where they spawn, or lay their eggs. The young, newly hatched dourada then travel back to the nurs-

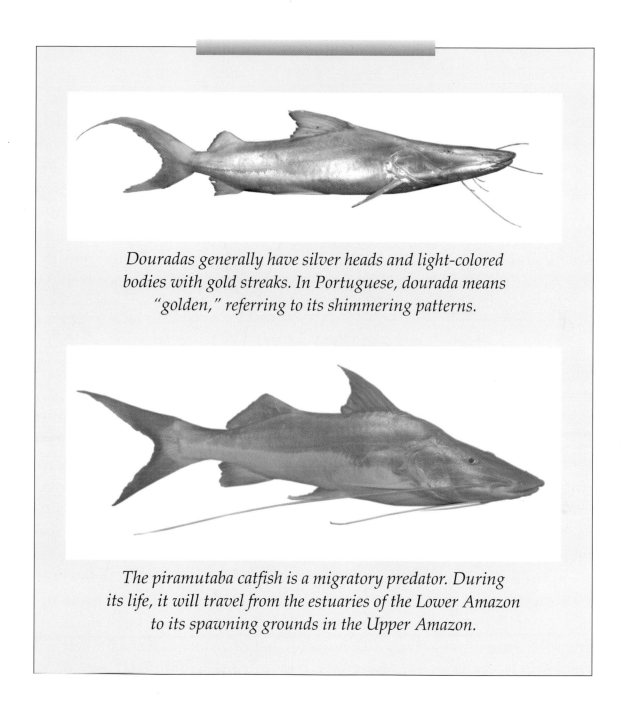

Douradas generally have silver heads and light-colored bodies with gold streaks. In Portuguese, dourada means "golden," referring to its shimmering patterns.

The piramutaba catfish is a migratory predator. During its life, it will travel from the estuaries of the Lower Amazon to its spawning grounds in the Upper Amazon.

ery habitat in the Lower Amazon estuaries, and the cycle begins again.

The piramutaba catfish is half the size of the dourada, seldom growing to more than 3 feet (1 m) in length or exceeding 15 to 20 pounds (6.8–9.1 kg) in weight. A two-tone fish with a gray back and a white belly, it is

found throughout the Middle and Lower Amazon. Although the piramutaba thrives in all three classes of rivers, it prefers the sediment-rich whitewater rivers. When water levels of the Lower Amazon are high and the estuaries are flooded with freshwater, large piramutaba take advantage of the abundance of prey fish found there. When the floodwaters retreat, however, and the salt water returns, both adults and preadults school together and migrate upriver. It takes approximately five months for them to reach the Upper Amazon where they spawn in the muddy rivers. Young as well as adult piramutaba then migrate together back to the estuaries.

An Aquatic Chameleon

While catfish have been the most important species to be exported from the Amazon Basin, it is a member of the characins that has been of primary importance in Amazonian markets and in feeding the local inhabitants. Characin are an incredibly diverse group in size, shape, and behavior. There are more than 1,200 species in Central and South America, as compared to about 200 species in Africa. As with so many other animal groups, the greatest diversity of characin is found in the Amazon Basin. Many popular aquarium fish, such as the tetras, are characins, as are the fabled piranhas.

One of the most common characins and a fish of great value to the rain forest is the tambaqui (TOM-bah-kee). It is a large fish that can grow up to 3 feet long (0.9 m) and weigh 50 to 60 pounds (22.7–27.2 kg). One of its special features is that the adult is somewhat of a slow-acting chameleon, changing its color in response to the type of water it inhabits. In muddy waters tambaquis are light or yellowish in color. In clearwater rivers they are two toned—light gray on top and almost black on the lower half. In blackwater rivers the entire body turns dark. This adaptation helps it blend in and avoid predators.

In addition to its powers of camouflage, the tambaqui sports an un-

An oval-shaped fish, tambaqui weighing up to 100 pounds (45.3 kg) were once frequently caught by anglers. Today, due to the increased pressures of fishing, it would be a rarity to catch one that size.

usual mouthful of teeth. This oddball has large squarish molars that would look more appropriate on a horse or a cow. These teeth are highly functional, though, well suited for crushing, cracking, and chewing seeds and fruits.

Although the tambaqui eats a variety of fruits and seeds that fall into the waters of the flooded forests, it targets two foods in particular—jauari palm fruits and the seeds of the rubber tree. The reason for such a specialized diet is that these tree species are widespread and produce large numbers of high-protein fruits and seeds. The hard shells of the rubber tree seeds may also eliminate other fish from eating them as their teeth are not as strong as the tambaqui's. Thus competition for this particular

Tambaqui are well suited for foraging the flooded forests. In addition to their powerful jaws and strong teeth, a highly developed sense of smell guides them to the fruits that have fallen into the water.

food is greatly reduced. Tambaqui are also sharp sighted, an adaptation that helps them snap up fruit, often as soon as it hits the water. Groups of them have been known to gather beneath a palm or rubber tree waiting for its fruit to fall. Some scientists believe that the fish can even recognize these trees by their submerged trunks.

The tambaqui has coevolved with the flooded forest, with the result that it acts in response to the seasonal rhythms of the floods. The relationship between the tambaqui and the flooded forest is a mutualistic one, meaning that they benefit each other. Many of the seeds the tambaqui eats pass through the fish without harm and are capable of sprouting and growing after they are excreted. Thus the tambaqui helps disperse the seeds. They often carry them to new habitats, expanding the range of the trees whose fruits they prefer. In return, the fish are provided with a nutritious diet and an increased habitat in which to search for food during the flood season.

The tambaqui is common in the Middle and Upper Amazon, found from west of the Xingu River to the Andes. But it is generally absent from the estuaries and rivers of eastern Amazonia. Its preferred habitats are the flooded forests and floodplain lakes. Although found in other types of waters, the tambaqui is most closely linked to the whitewater rivers whose associated floodplain lakes serve as their primary nursery habitats.

When water levels are low, these characins no longer have access to the bounty of the forest. Then they remain in the river channels living off their stored fat. Trees along the riverbanks that have fallen into the water due to eroded banks serve as important refuge habitats. When it is time to spawn, at the beginning of the flood season, tambaquis lay their eggs at the edges of sediment-rich rivers and their tributaries. After spawning, adults scatter, heading back to the waters of the floodplains. Eggs and fry drift downriver. Whitewater floodplain lakes serve as nursery habitats for the young for about four years. At that age, the tambaqui migrate to the river channels.

Predatory piranhas often live in schools, or groups, but also hunt alone. Tales of their aggressive nature are greatly exaggerated.

Chapter Five

UNDERWATER HUNTERS

*T*he piranha is probably the best-known characin. It is found throughout the northern half of the continent. There are many species, with twenty to twenty-five found in the waters of the Amazon Basin. Exaggerated accounts of piranha attacks have filled explorers' journals and adventure tales for the past two hundred years. Travelers have offered their own fanciful reports, adding to the piranha's fierce reputation. The truth about their aggressive feeding habits is much less sensational.

Piranhas do not pose any threat to people in moving water such as rivers and streams. People who live near the Amazon bathe daily along the riverbanks as their children play in the water. In the Peruvian Amazon I have watched my guide fish from a floating dock and catch a piranha while people were swimming 20 feet (6.1 m) away. While these fish normally do not present a danger, there are circumstances where piranhas could behave like the vicious predators they are made out to be.

If piranhas are living in a lake or large pool of water that has been depleted of prey, they are likely to attack anything. We have seen how the rivers rise seasonally to flood the surrounding forests on the floodplain. If a group of piranhas became trapped in one of these flooded areas as the waters receded, they would attack and eat anything there to survive. Only under these extreme circumstances when the fish are facing starvation could there be any truth to their mythical reputation.

The red piranha, although seldom reaching more than
8 inches (20.3 cm) in length, is a well-equipped predator
with a strong jaw filled with sharp, triangular teeth.

Piranhas typically live in small groups and do not seem to migrate. The average piranha is less than 1 foot (30 cm) long, although some may grow up to 20 inches (51 cm) and weigh as much as 4 pounds (1.8 kg). Most are almost diamond shaped, similar in profile to the tambaqui. One look in the mouth however, will eliminate any confusion between the two. The piranha's jaws are lined with triangular, razor-sharp teeth, making it perfectly equipped for its role as a predator.

Piranhas have evolved a variety of feeding strategies. Each species seems to have preferred foods, but they are opportunistic, meaning they

consume whatever comes along. Examinations of the contents of their stomachs have revealed that most piranhas eat a variety of foods. Some stomachs have contained fish as well as seeds, beetles, crabs, birds, and lizards. The carnivores, or meat eaters, often lurk, dart out, bite off a piece of their prey, then retreat. Some even specialize in attacking the fins of other fish, while others concentrate on the scales.

Other piranhas are seed specialists, having been found with stomachs full of ground-up seeds. It seems unusual to think of piranhas that are herbivores, yet that is the case—most of the time. However, even the stomachs of seed eaters have been shown to contain fish parts, while seeds may comprise as much as 10 percent of the diet of those species that primarily consume meat. It is also possible that the diet of some species changes seasonally in response to the relative abundance and availability of food. Thus, the seed-eating piranhas are actually adaptable omnivores, able to consume both plants and other animals.

Bony Tongues

Piranhas share the basin's rivers with an ancient group represented by only three species in all of South America. Two of these species, the pirarucu (PEE-rah-ROO-koo) and the aruana (AH-roo-WAH-nuh), have developed, through adaptation, their own unique anatomical features. With their long heavy bodies, flat backs like a moray eel, and small heads, they are easy to recognize. They belong to the osteoglossid family, which means "bony tongue." They get their names from their toothed and rasp-like tongues.

The pirarucu is a giant Amazonian predator found in all types of rivers and especially in quiet whitewater floodplain lakes. It is one of the largest tropical freshwater fish and can reach a length of 10 feet (3 m) and weigh more than 300 pounds (136 kg). But today few specimens even approaching this size are caught, as the pirarucu has been a favorite food fish for decades. The original inhabitants of the floodplains used to hunt the

As big as a man, the pirarucu (left) is one of the Amazon's largest fresh-water fish. This giant was caught in a gill net near Santarem, Brazil.

Although known for its spectacular jumping ability, the aruana (below) generally swims just beneath the water's surface, feeding on the variety of organisms it finds there. Because they swallow their prey whole, aruanas do not have any teeth.

pirarucu with wooden harpoons from a dugout canoe. This enormous fish has the unusual trait of breathing air rather than getting its oxygen from the water. Therefore it must come to the surface from time to time for breath. The hunters would wait, their harpoons poised, attentive to the slightest rippling of the water's surface and any sign of the massive fish surfacing.

The aruana, or water monkey, looks like a smaller, more streamlined version of the pirarucu, but seldom grows to more than 3 feet (0.9 m) in length. It has a large mouth that it uses for grabbing and gulping prey. This member of the bony-tongued fishes is a mouth breeder and produces only a small number of eggs. The male keeps them in his mouth where they are protected and have a better chance of surviving. It guards the young for a short period as well, after hatching them in his mouth.

The nickname water monkey is applied with good reason. Although aruanas are predators, fish evidently form only a small part of their diet. The majority of prey consists of insects and other arthropods, especially beetles and spiders. These fish will sometimes jump almost twice their body length out of the water to snag an insect from an overhanging branch. These acrobatics, more like an agile monkey than a fish, have helped earn this creature its nickname. Although many have witnessed these spectacular displays, the aruana's most common approach to feeding is to gulp down insects that have fallen in the water. All in all, the aruana is not picky. Even birds, bats, and snakes have been found in their stomachs.

The aruana is not typically a river resident. During low-water periods it gathers in floodplain lakes. During high water, it spreads into the flooded forest. In both habitats it is often seen near the water's edge, which is the best place to forage for fallen insects.

A triggerlike mechanism in the anhinga's neck allows it to propel its bill rapidly forward and spear a nearby fish. Sometimes its thrust is so powerful, the anhinga has to remove its catch by using a rock onshore.

Chapter Six

LINKS IN THE CHAIN

With so many fish in the Amazon Basin, it is not surprising that they help feed the countless organisms that live in and along its waters. Amphibians, reptiles, birds, and mammals all take their place in a complex web of connections. No animal exists in a world of its own. Rather, all of the basin's residents affect each other, helping or harming their chances for survival. One way the Amazon's plants and animals are linked is through the many food chains the region supports. A bird, an anhinga, eats a fish, a dourada. The anhinga is, in turn, snatched by a snake, the massive anaconda. The energy contained in the fish is passed to the bird and then, in turn, to the snake. But this is just an example of one of the basin's feeding relationships. There are countless numbers of food chains that bind the region's various species.

The matamata turtle is a river resident whose primitive appearance seems more from the time of the dinosaurs. It is a bottom dweller that awaits its prey in shallow, peaceful waters. Its brown color and unusual shape allow it to blend in with a stream bottom. As a small fish swims by, it quickly opens its mouth and dilates, or expands, its throat. This results in water and the prey being sucked in, a technique also used by many of the Amazon's catfish. A slender, snorkel-like nose allows this predator to stretch its long neck to the surface so it can breathe and remain motionless underwater. The most remarkable thing about the matamata however is its appearance. Its shell looks bumpy and rocky while its head is

flattened with strange flanges and projections. It does not look like a turtle, or any other animal for that matter.

The Amazon region does not have crocodiles, but it does have caimans (KAY-mins), its version of the alligator. Like many of the Amazon's turtle species, both the black and the spectacled caiman were formerly plentiful along the river and its tributaries. They were hunted, primarily for their skins. The smaller spectacled caiman only reaches a length of 8 feet (2.5 m), but the black caiman can attain the impressive size of 20 feet (6 m). Although few caiman this size are seen any more, I have frequently observed the "eye shine" of smaller individuals at night. Searching from an open boat with a flashlight, the glowing red reflection from their eyes sticking out of the water lets you know there are caiman in the vicinity. At the top of the food chain, few animals can threaten an adult caiman other than people or perhaps the anaconda.

The anaconda is the largest snake in the world. One of these giant constrictors measured just less than 38 feet (11.4 m) and more than 500 pounds (225 kg). The anaconda feeds on a range of small and large mam-

The matamata turtle is typically found camouflaged in a streambed. Its strangely distorted head ends in a long, snorkel-like nose.

Seldom found far from the water, the anaconda is an excellent swimmer. It generally prefers shallow water, where it waits for passing prey.

mals, as well as birds. Also known as the water boa, it throws its coils around its prey and squeezes it, killing it by suffocation. The victim is then swallowed whole. Various other boas, including the boa constrictor and the spectacularly colored emerald tree boa, share the flooded forest with the anaconda. However, these other species generally stay in the trees, while the anaconda is never far from the water.

Sometimes the best way to travel the waters of the Amazon Basin is in a small, open boat. That way it is possible to enter one of the small oxbow lakes and see one of the Amazon's most unique bird species. A series of low grunts warns you that you are getting close to what the local people call the "stink bird," but what is better known as the hoatzin.

The hoatzin is about the size of a chicken and a very poor flyer. It is commonly found along the edges of lakes, hopping clumsily among the branches. It has a small head with a large crest and blue skin surrounding its red beady eyes. One of the traits that makes the hoatzin unique is that it is the world's only leaf-eating bird. More than 80 percent of its diet consists

The hoatzin is typically found along the edges of lakes. It is an arboreal species. Although it occasionally flies in a slow, clumsy manner, it prefers to climb among the branches of trees.

of leaves, primarily from a large plant with arrowhead-shaped leaves that belongs to the philodendron family. These leaves contain chemicals that make the hoatzins distasteful or poisonous to most other animals.

Once eaten, the leaf pieces go to a double organ in the hoatzin's diges-
tive system called a crop. They are held in the crop where special bacteria
cause them to ferment. This process is similar to cows and other rumi-
nants that also rely on a leafy diet. It is the fermentation process that
ensures the leaves' chemicals do not harm the hoatzin. It also gives the
hoatzin's meat an unpleasant taste, resulting in the unflattering nickname stink bird. This adaptation has been particularly beneficial, pre-
venting this clumsy bird from being hunted to extinction.

The hoatzin's odd qualities do not end with its feeding habits. They
build simple nests of sticks in plants growing from the water. At a sign of
alarm, a chick or young hoatzin will jump out of the nest and into the water
to hide among the tangled bases of plants. When danger has passed, the
young hoatzins use claws on their wings to climb back into the nest. These
claws are found on the juveniles of this species and on no other birds.

You might not typically expect to mistake a bird for a snake, yet there is
one Amazon bird with which this could easily happen. Known as the
anhinga, it is also appropriately called the "snake bird." A predator that
feeds mostly on fish, the anhinga frequents rivers, lakes, and swamps.
The fish are speared on its pointed bill. The anhinga often swims underwater with just its long, thin neck visible above the surface, moving like a
snake in the water. Like a cormorant, this bird can often be seen perched
in the sun with its wings extended as it dries its feathers.

These are just a few of the animals that take their place in the Amazon's
many connecting and overlapping food chains. Just as the Amazon Basin
is more than a single channel of water, the rivers of the region are not
home solely to the world of fish. The rivers act as crossroads, drawing
species from the ocean, the air, and the surrounding forest.

The river basin is just one of the places where all the various food
chains combine to form a vast network of feeding relationships known as
a food web. Organisms need to eat in order to survive. The rivers of the
basin are one of the places where this essential activity is played out.

Floating meadows form seasonally when the whitewater rivers flood their banks. These floating mats of grass and aquatic plants are an extremely important, but often overlooked, habitat in the Amazon Basin.

Chapter Seven

MEADOWS THAT FLOAT

A s the Amazon and its whitewater tributaries flood each year, a new ecological community forms throughout the basin. For their relatively small size, these habitats are incredibly rich in life and harbor thriving communities of plants and animals. They also provide grazing grounds for the Amazon's largest mammal and the world's largest rodent. Called floating meadows, these tangled islands of grasses, aquatic plants, and dangling roots provide shelter and feeding grounds for many Amazonian species.

Floating meadows are mats of living vegetation that form in nutrient-rich waters. Although they sometimes sprout in blackwater and clearwater tributaries, they are more commonly found in the muddy whitewater rivers and their associated lakes. They grow in the quiet waters along riverbanks or the shallow portions of lakes, thriving in areas of open sunlight. Sometimes they remain rooted to the river bottom or the lakebed, while in other cases they become free-floating islands that may cover as much as a square mile.

It is not surprising that a number of species found among these plant islands have the word *water* in their name. Water lily, water hyacinth, and water lettuce join sedges, ferns, and broadleaf plants to form large, floating meadows. One of the main grasses is a species called pemembeca. It leads a double life, adapted for both aquatic and terrestrial habitats. During high-water season it is a fast-growing floating plant that spreads quickly. At the time of year when the water is low, seeds from its flowers germinate in the freshly deposited sediments. However as a land plant, pemembeca has a much different look than its aquatic alter-ego.

The giant Amazon water lily, sometimes called the Queen Victoria lily, is among the floating meadow's most impressive plants. Often found at the edge of lakes, it remains rooted to the muddy bottom and must grow to keep pace with the rising level of the water. Its huge floating leaves may measure 6 feet (1.8 m) in diameter and are covered with sharp spines on the underside. The large showy 6-inch (15.2-cm) flower is white at first, but turns pink after being pollinated by scarab beetles that are lured by the flower's fragrance and then trapped into spending the night inside the closed blossom.

Floating meadows provide important habitats for a number of aquatic animals. It offers, as an alternative to the land, a place to perch or hunt for animals, such as frogs and snakes, that live above water. However, it is just as important to the aquatic creatures that find shelter among the partially submerged grass stems and the maze of dangling roots that fill the water below. For it is beneath the water's surface that a variety of insect larvae, crabs, freshwater shrimp, and fry are found.

At times, I have entered the interior of a floating meadow in a canoe. While resting from the supreme effort needed to force the canoe among the tangled plants, I have been amazed at the number of insects and arachnids I have observed. The air above these floating plants is alive with dragonflies and damselflies, some seeking mates, others hunting prey, and still others defending territories they have staked out for themselves. The surface of the meadow is crawling with grasshoppers, spiders, caterpillars, weevils, and many other arthropods that may live their entire lives within the meadow's confines. The underside of the meadow houses just as many, if not more, of these small invertebrates. These include the predatory larvae of the dragonflies and damselflies seen flying above, mosquito larvae attached to the plant roots, and a variety of crustaceans. All of these crea-

Water lettuce floats tightly packed among the larger pads
of the giant Amazon water lily. The dangling roots of these
and other plants that make up a floating meadow are host to
a variety of organisms that serve as food for young fish.

Capybaras spend much of their time in small groups in or near the water. They communicate with each other using a combination of whistles, barks, and scent from the male's glands.

tures provide food for the large schools of young fish.

Fish are vulnerable when they are young. They easily fall prey to larger fish and many other predators, both aquatic and terrestrial. Thus, floating meadows are important communities that provide fry a relatively safe haven where they can both feed and develop. Many of the flooded forest's

fruit-eating species, including the tambaqui, use the floating meadows as nurseries. Some scientists think that one of the reasons migratory fish leave blackwater and clearwater habitats for whitewater rivers is to provide the hatchling fish with the food and protection the floating meadows offer.

Meadow Mammals

Two unique species are frequent visitors to these incredibly rich habitats. The capybara and the manatee are the only native mammals to graze floating meadows. Capybaras look like sleepy, overgrown guinea pigs. At 4 feet (1.2 m) long and 130 pounds (60 kg), they are the world's largest rodent. Capybaras spend much of their time in the water where they feed on aquatic plants. Their feet are partially webbed, which helps them move about in the marshy environments they frequent. Capybaras usually stay in family groups of six to eight individuals, but have been known to live in herds totaling fifty to sixty. Floating meadows draw them as a rich source of food. But increased pressure through hunting and the spread of towns and villages has altered this rodent's typical behavior. Formerly a common sight in the Amazon Basin, some capybaras are fast becoming reclusive.

The Amazonian manatee is the largest resident of the basin's waterways. This docile mammal can weigh up to 1,100 pounds (500 kg) and reach a length of 9 feet (2.8 m). It looks much like a walrus without its tusks and is the only plant-eating mammal to live exclusively in freshwater. Feeding only on aquatic vegetation, the manatee is the primary consumer. Although extremely rare now, it is sometimes found in quiet waters where water hyacinth and water lettuce grow. Although the manatee's size may be intimidating, it is by nature a gentle animal. It has no natural aquatic predators, but it is now threatened with extinction due to decades of being hunted for its meat, oil, and skin. It is a lucky Amazon visitor who witnesses the face of a manatee surface among a thick mat of water hyacinth to take a breath of air and munch a mouthful of floating plants.

Although floating meadows are a tangled nuisance for some boat travelers, they are important seasonal habitats for the many organisms drawn there. Part land, part river, they are wet worlds that house, hide, and feed.

Weighing more than half a ton, the Amazonian
manatee is the largest animal found in the basin's rivers.
Although it has no natural aquatic predators, overhunting
by the Amazon's human residents has now placed it
on the endangered species list.

Floating meadows undergo a natural cycle of growth and decay, but cattle ranching in riverside pastures has led in recent years to the trampling and destruction of those found near riverbanks. In addition, the water buffalo, a foreign species now being raised in parts of Amazonia, graze the meadows before they have had time to fully develop, robbing many animals of this unique habitat. As in any biological community, change is unavoidable. But it is not necessarily good.

The waters of the Amazon Basin are home to more specie of fish than anywhe else. Although this resource was once thought to be unlimited, catches have dropped drastically in recen years due to increased fishing.

Chapter Eight

RESOURCE FOR THE FUTURE

*T*he Amazon is the lifeline of northern South America in more ways than one. Beyond the array of highly adapted plants and animals it supports, there is another complex organism whose survival often depends on the river as well—people. Several species of fish have helped feed most of Amazonia for hundreds of years. Catching, processing, and transporting thc fish are a huge industry that provides many jobs. Today, however, the yields are down. Rarely given the time to achieve maturity, the fish themselves are smaller. Overfishing has finally affected what once seemed like an endless supply of animal protein. Deforestation, pollution, and the ecological damage caused by large hydroelectric dams constructed along Amazonian rivers have all resulted in the loss of essential habitat as well.

Once, the Amazon has seemed like an unlimited resource. However, several factors have changed that. In the 1970s, fishing boats were first modernized, equipped with refrigeration and large nets. This made it possible to take in greater catches with little loss from spoilage. The construction of roads to some of the major cities in southern Brazil allowed refrigerated trucks to transport large shipments of fish to areas that were once difficult to reach. Together, such improvements in technology and transportation have led to fish being shipped to both international and

Inhabitants of the Amazon who use traditional methods, such as a bow and arrow, have little effect on the fish populations.

domestic markets. As a result, the populations of Amazonian fish have been greatly reduced.

The piramutaba catfish has been the species most heavily exploited for export. Some years, more than 25,000 tons (22,680 metric tons) were reported taken, with approximately 70 percent of the fish going to export. Industrial fleets fishing the estuaries and the Lower Amazon bring their refrigerated catches to packing plants in Belém at the mouth of the Amazon. Here the fish are processed and flown, shipped, or trucked to their various markets. Large piramutaba catches are also made in the Middle Amazon where they are frozen at refrigeration plants in cities such as Manaus. They are then brought by barge to Belém for processing and distribution.

The dourada is also taken in great numbers from Amazonian estuaries. Since this is the nursery habitat of this species, overfishing the estuaries could decimate the juvenile populations. As the fish has a wide distribution, dourada are caught by commercial fleets as well as local fishermen throughout the Amazon Basin, from the river's mouth as far west as Peru and Colombia. But due to their predictable migrations, dourada are also taken from the inland rivers of the Middle and Upper Amazon. For example, fishermen in the *tres fronteras* area deliver catches to the Colombian jungle port of Leticia, where they are frozen and flown to the capital of Bogotá. Even in the Peruvian jungle city of Pucallpa along the Ucayali River more than 2,000 miles (3,219 km) from the estuaries of the Amazon, dourada is one of the main fish in the markets.

The widespread characin, the tambaqui, however, offers the hope of change and improved methods of harvesting. In the 1970s, tambaqui represented almost half of all the fish sold in the Middle Amazon. Although it still accounts for a very large portion of the fish catch, today, like most other species, juveniles are being sold rather than adults. This is a clear indication that the decades of heavy fishing have taken their toll.

The increasing demand for this fish has also affected its price. It is now too expensive for many of the people who catch it, costing as much or more than beef. In many places, it is now consumed only by wealthier families or used for export. Although this is distressing to the poorer people of the Amazon, the great value of tambaqui meat may provide new opportunities for rainforest conservation.

The tambaqui offers hope for the preservation of the Amazon rain for-

Aquaculture efforts, such as the fish farm that produced this tambaqui, may prove to be more profitable and less destructive to the rainforest ecosystem than herding cattle. Conservation programs could look to these other methods of producing meat.

est because it could be cultured, or raised, in a less destructive manner than cattle, yet with similar meat yields and financial gains. In place of cutting down trees to create pastureland, "fish orchards" of trees that produce the seeds and fruits eaten by the tambaqui could be planted, intermixed with the original trees. These orchards, along with protecting existing food trees and floodplain habitats, would help preserve the forest. In addition, the tambaqui has lent itself to a small, but growing aquaculture industry. Currently this adaptable fish is being raised in ponds, both in and outside of the Amazon Basin. It has the potential of being one of the few native Amazonian animals that could compete with cattle in meat production.

Fish are tied to the health and well-being of the Amazon ecosystem and the people that inhabit it. Overfishing in the Lower Amazon affects catches in the headwaters on the other side of the continent. Likewise, should the spawning areas in the muddy rivers of the Upper Amazon be damaged or rendered unusable, fish populations in the estuary could disappear. Long-distance fish migrations often span thousands of miles and occur in more than one country. The Amazon is a vast interconnected world filled with countless habitats and environments that stretch from its estuaries near the Atlantic Ocean to its headwaters in the Andes. Conservationists and government officials must consider the whole Amazon region if they are going to preserve the river, its tributaries, its flooded forests, and the tremendous diversity of life they house.

GLOSSARY

adaptation: a change in appearance, behavior, or biology that increases an organism's chance of surviving.

aquaculture: the captive breeding and raising of aquatic animals such as fish or shrimp.

barbels: slender, feelerlike sense organs located near the mouths of catfish.

biodiversity: the variety of all living organisms found within a given area or habitat (such as a rain forest).

blackwater river: a river such as the Negro whose waters are dark and tea colored due to tannins and organic compounds.

carnivore: an organism that feeds on meat or animal material.

cichlid: a family of fishes containing the most important group of predatory fish used for food in Amazonia.

clearwater river: a nutrient-poor river such as the Xingu that carries almost no sediment, resulting in the water being nearly transparent.

competition: a situation where two or more organisms are vying for the same resource (such as food, a nesting site, or a prospective mate).

confluence: the point at which two or more rivers come together.

estuary: a freshwater, often coastal, waterway that is subject to invasion by salt water from the tides. In the Amazon Basin, this occurs between the mouth of the Xingu River and the Atlantic Ocean.

floating meadow: a seasonal ecological community that consists of floating and aquatic plants and grasses that serve as a nursery habitat for young and developing fish.

flooded forest: also known as floodplain forest or seasonally inundated forest, a wooded area that becomes flooded for a certain period each year.

floodplain: the area on either side of a river that becomes submerged when the water rises and overflows the banks.

food chain: a series of feeding relationships in which organisms are linked by one eating the other.

habitat: the physical place or area in which a creature lives.

headwaters: the area or location where a river begins.

igapó: a forest that occurs on the floodplains of blackwater rivers.

inundation: a flood.

Lower Amazon: the part of the Amazon Basin that extends east or downstream from the Brazilian city of Santarém to the coast.

Middle Amazon: the part of the Amazon Basin located almost entirely within Brazil that extends west from the city of Santarém to the city of Tefé.

migratory: using habitats in different locations at different times; traveling from an established location in order to mate or find additional food.

mutualism: a relationship between two different species that live in direct contact with one another, both benefiting from the relationship.

nursery habitat: an area where young fish feed and develop, such as a floating meadow.

omnivore: an organism that feeds on both plant and animal material.

opportunistic: feeding on one type of material or prey, but eating a different type of food if it is presented.

organism: a living creature.

precipitation: weather events such as rain or snow that lead to water being added to the land.

predator: an organism that preys and feeds on animals.

spawn: in fish, the act of mating and releasing fertilized eggs.

tannin: a chemical compound found in plants that is released into the soil as leaves fall and decompose.

terra firma: a type of forest that is never flooded.

temperate: a climatic zone characterized by mild weather and distinct seasons.

terrestrial: land based, such as an organism that lives on land.

tributary: a waterway that branches off from the main river or channel.

Upper Amazon: that part of the Amazon Basin that extends from the Brazilian city of Tefé west to the Andes Mountains.

várzea: forests that occur on the floodplains of whitewater rivers.

whitewater river: nutrient-rich rivers such as the Amazon or the Madeira that are muddy and brown in color due to the extensive amount of sediment they carry.

SPECIES AT A GLANCE

Amazonian Manatee *(Trichechus inunguis):* The largest native Amazonian mammal and animal. This large aquatic, walruslike animal feeds on leafy aquatic plants. Once plentiful, it is now endangered due to overhunting for its meat and hide.

Anaconda *(Eunectes murinus):* The largest Amazonian snake and reptile. Always associated with water, anacondas prey on birds and mammals that they kill by constriction.

Anhinga *(Anhinga anhinga):* A cormorant-like bird with a long, slender neck and fan-shaped tail. Anhingas spear fish with their bill and are known as "snake birds" because they swim in the water with just their head and neck exposed.

Aruana *(Osteoglossum bicirrhosum):* A long, fish with a large mouth that can reach 3 feet (1 m) in length. Often seen at the edges of lakes and flooded forests, the aruana has been called the "water monkey" due to its ability to leap clear of the water to snatch insects from low-hanging branches.

Caiman: Alligator-like reptiles that inhabit Amazonian rivers and lakes. Once abundant, hunting has decimated populations of the black caiman *(Melanosuchus niger)* and the smaller spectacled caiman *(Caiman crocodilus).*

Capybara *(Hydrochaeris hydrochaeris):* A semi-aquatic mammal that is also the world's largest rodent. With the appearance of a large guinea pig, capybaras feed on aquatic plants and spend much of their time partially submerged in water.

Dourada *(Brachyplatystoma flavicans):* A large, migratory Amazon catfish that reaches 60 pounds (27.2 kg) in weight. Its name means "golden," referring to the gold-colored tint of the body.

Giant Amazon Water Lily *(Victoria amazonica):* An aquatic plant with a typical water lily flower and a floating pad that is spiny underneath and can reach a diameter of 6 feet (1.8 m). It is found in areas of quiet water along the edges of lakes and as part of floating meadows.

Hoatzin *(Opisthocomus hoazin):* A clumsy-flying, crested, chicken-sized bird that inhabits floodplain lakes and feeds on leaves. The young have claws on the wings and plunge in the water to escape predators.

Pemembeca *(Paspalum repens):* A species of floating grass that is one of the main components of the plant communities found in floating meadows. It is quick growing and has both an aquatic and terrestrial form.

Piramutaba (*Brachyplatystoma vailantii*): A migratory catfish that reaches 3 feet (1 m) in length and 20 pounds (9.1 kg) in weight. It is heavily fished commercially for exportation.

Piranha (*Serrasalmus spp.*): A group of fish with sharp triangular teeth represented by 20–25 species in the Amazon Basin. They display a variety of feeding preferences, including food items such as fish, fruit, and invertebrates. Large predatory species such as the red piranha (*S. natteri*) are popularly and falsely believed to attack anything that enters the water.

Pirarucu (*Arapaima gigas*): A giant flat-bodied fish with a small head that breathes air. Found especially in quiet whitewater lakes, it may reach up to 10 feet (3 m) in length and 300 pounds (136 kg) in weight.

Tambaqui (*Colossoma macropomum*): An important migratory, fruit-feeding fish of the flooded forest with distinctive molarlike teeth. It is one of the most important food fish to the people of Amazonia.

Water Hyacinth (*Eichornia crassipes*): An aquatic plant with beautiful pink hyacinth-like flowers and swollen stems that aid it in floating. Often one of the species found in floating meadows.

Water Lettuce (*Pistia stratiotes*): A floating aquatic plant with light green squarish leaves that grow in a rosette and long dangling roots. It often forms dense carpets on the surfaces of quiet lakes and in areas where there are floating meadows.

FIND OUT MORE

BOOKS

Blue, Rose, and Naden, Corinne J. *Andes Mountains.* Austin, TX: Raintree Steck-Vaughn, 1994.

Grossman, Susan. *Piranhas.* Parsippany, NJ: Silver Burdett, 1996.

Kallen, Stuart A. *Life in the Amazon Rain-Forest.* San Diego: Lucent, 1999.

McAuliffe, Emily. *Piranhas.* Danbury, CT: Franklin Watts, 1997.

Pirotta, Saviour. *Rivers in the Rain Forest.* Austin, TX: Raintree Steck-Vaughn, 1999.

Pinkguni, Manolito. *Piranhas.* Broomall, PA: Chelsea House, 1999.

Pollard, Michael. *The Amazon.* New York: Benchmark Books, 1997.

These books for older readers might be helpful as well:

Araujo-Lima, Carlos, and Michael Goulding. *So Fruitful a Fish.* New York: Columbia University Press, 1997.

Barthem, Ronaldo, and Michael Goulding. *The Catfish Connection.* New York: Columbia University Press, 1997.

Goulding, Michael. *The Fishes and the Forest.* Berkeley: University of California Press, 1980.

Smith, Nigel J.H. *Man, Fishes, and the Amazon.* New York: Columbia University Press, 1981.

WEBSITES

Amazon Catfish
ww.acuteangling.com/Catfish/Cathome.html

The Amazon River
ww.mbarron.net/Amazon/

Amazon's Depth Reveal Strange New World of Unknown Fish
www.keil.ukans.edu/%7Eneodat/amazon-sci.html

American Society of Ichthyologists and Herpetologists
www.utexas.edu/depts/asih/

Database of Fish Diversity in the Neotropics
www.neodat.org/

Enchanted Learning: Rain Forests
www.enchantedlearning.com/Home.html

Fish Diversity of the Principal Channels of the Amazon River
http://eebweb.arizona.edu/fish/cal-hamaz.html

Neotropical Ichthyological Association
www.pucrs.br/museu/nia

Project Piaba
www.angelfire.com/pq/piaba

Preservation of the Amazonian River Dolphin
www.isptr-pard.org/

World of Piranhas
www.piranha.org/

ORGANIZATIONS

Conservation International
2501 M Street NW Suite 200
Washington, D.C. 20037
(800) 406-2306
www.conservation.org

Cultural Survival
215 Prospect Street
Cambridge, MA 02139
(617) 441-5400
www.cs.org

Friends of the Earth
1025 Vermont Ave. NW
Washington, D.C. 20005-6303
(877) 843-8687 or (202) 783-7400
www.foe.org

National Wildlife Federation
8925 Leesburg Pike
Vienna, VA 22184
(703) 790-4000
www.nwf.org/nwf

Nature Conservancy
4245 North Fairfax Drive, Suite 100
Arlington, VA 22203-1606
(800) 628-6860
www.tnc.org

Rainforest Action Network
221 Pine Street, Suite 500
San Francisco, CA 94104
(415) 398-4404
www.ran.org

Rainforest Alliance
65 Bleeker Street
New York, N.Y. 10012-2420
(212) 677-1900 or (800) MY EARTH
www.rainforest-alliance.org

World Wildlife Fund
1250 24th Street, NW
P.O. Box 97180
Washington, D.C. 20037
(800) CALL-WWF
www.worldwildlife.org

ABOUT THE AUTHOR

Dr. James L. Castner is a tropical biologist-writer-photographer and adjunct professor of biology at Pittsburg State University. He has traveled throughout the rain forests of South and Central America, but has focused primarily on the Amazon Basin of Peru. His main interest is how insects defend themselves, especially with the use of camouflage and mimicry. His unique photos of rainforest insects have appeared in *National Geographic*, *Natural History*, *International Wildlife*, *Ranger Rick*, and *Kids Discover* magazines.

Dr. Castner has spent the past several years writing books about insects and the rain forest. He often conducts educational workshops and leads students and teachers on visits to the Tropics. As part of his desire to work with younger students, he is completing his secondary certification in science and Spanish. He plans to finish his career teaching a combination of middle school, high school, and college students.

INDEX

*Page numbers in **boldface** indicate illustrations.*